Stories of the South
in free verse poetry

by Elliot M. Rubin

Copyright July 2019

Library of Congress

ISBN13 - 978-1-7328493-0-3

No part of this book may be reproduced in any form whatsoever without the prior, express written consent of the author.

This book is fiction, and all names, people, places, and happenings are from the author's imagination and are used fictionally.

Any resemblance to any living or dead persons, and/or businesses, locations and/or events is coincidental in its entirety.

All rights reserved

Dedication

To my darling Laura
for bearing with me all these years.

Preface

Free verse poetry allows a story to be told without rhyming or a mathematical structure restricting the flow of words.

This collection tells stories based on experiences, people, and situations I encountered on my travels in the South. For literary purposes, states, towns, and people have been combined into one location and story then fictionalized.

I hope you enjoy them.

.

Table of Contents

a southern town 7
the woods 9
The Joint 11
Saturday night at The Joint 12
buddies fishing by the creek 13
country pizza place 15
homemade lightning 16
the railroad station 18
home 20
in the beginning 21
as usual - Summer 24
fatback 25
that area of town 27
the big day 28
honeymoon fever 29
firehouse barbeque 30
Sunday services come weekly 31
small town standout 32
the law 33
school 34
a red mailbox 35
cold water 36
all spiffed up 37
Jesus 38
American whiskey 39
racing 40

yummy in your tummy 41

lunch 42

visiting New Jersey 43

farm life 45

Effie's House of Beauty - a true story 47

uniting families 48

small town sports 50

a southern town

Summer in the south-
Oppressive humidity,
stifling, while
a dog lies all day
on the cool, dry,
linoleum floor
in the kitchen
with no air-conditioning,
window fans
blowing in warm air
trying to evaporate
sweat from the
eyebrows of the
inhabitants inside

the town is small

in a central square
the county courthouse
is situated in the middle,
with green lawns
surrounding it
in springtime,
before turning brown
in the hot July sun

on three corners
of the square,
liquor stores
alleviate
the boredom
of living in the middle
of nowhere;
a pawn shop is

on the fourth corner
where folks get cash
for the other three corners

the town, located
in a valley
in the middle
of a Tennessee mountain range
filled with small villages,
small valleys,
all interchangeable,
an hour's drive away
for genetic diversity

driving through town
after the parade ended,
honoring the Strawberry Festival,
i spot old cars
mounted on cinder blocks
in the front and rear yards
where the locals intended
to work on them,
but never did.
a treasure trove
of America's
great manufacturing history
rusting away,
waiting for restoration
"someday"

the woods

every small town
in Appalachia has woods-
some larger,
some smaller,
all dense and thick
suitable for hunting deer
and little critters
when the season rolls around

the forest also hides
lovers
who park nearby
bringing blankets,
intending to escape
from prying eyes and ears;
hunting love not deer

a rural motel
with a lot of rooms
is located
a mile or so away
from the middle
of nowhere special;
off the state highway
which runs through town

used at night
by truckers
on their way
to someplace else,
they park their rigs
shoulder to shoulder
on the back dirt lot-

trailers help
block the sound
of the midnight
mile long freight trains
running next to the motel;
but can't prevent
the vibrations
of the steel wheels
on the iron tracks
shaking deep sleepers
despite their cozy beds

during the day
all trailers are gone;
only one or two cars
are parked in back;
lonely local wives
meeting their lovers
while husbands
are driving a big rig
to somewhere
out of town

The Joint

the narrow
two-lane bypass
mirrors
the interstate,
through lush green valleys-
picturesque small churches
set back from the road
against forest and foliage

a few miles before
town is The Joint-
BBQ,
line dancing,
good home cooking,
with country music
playing from noon
till people leave
for home
or work

Saturday night at The Joint

in a back moonlit
parking lot,
after a night of booze,
hard-hitting live music,
DNA mingles
repopulating
the area-
with cousins,
shotgun marriages,
adultery,
and unmentionable relationships
sometimes playing out
in future misery

buddies fishing by the creek

walking to the creek
to go fishing
the shade
of the forest
somewhat cools
hot summer air

after years
of experience
they found
their good spot-
a ways before
the creek turns
to merge
with the flowing river

they set their lures-
then cast
into calm water
near rocks
and water lilies

setting the poles
into tubes
stuck in the ground,
they sit,
open a bottle
of bourbon
brought to share,
to kill time,
to be social,
waiting…
for the fish to bite

when the liquor
is finished,
love making
is finished,
fishing lines
wound in,
tubes pulled up,
empty bag to store fish
closed,
they wobble back
on the path
through the woods
to waiting
trucks,

air conditioning,

   silence,

      sleeping it off

country pizza place

a visitor to the area
decided one night
to visit the local
franchise pizza place
on Main Street

a young waitress walks over,
pizza is ordered,
a side salad too

*can i have oil and vinegar
on the salad please*

*we have oil…
is vinegar the red stuff?*

yes

no, we don't have it.

at least the pizza is hot

homemade lightning

walking down
a steep hillside
to the bottom
of the gully
he can spot,
through the dense
overgrowth below,
old rusted barrels
sitting in a row

tubes flowing
out the tops
where good ol' boys
use to make
quality moonshine

his daddy
made the still
years ago,
during the twenties-
prohibition didn't exist
in these parts of the country

with a car full of hooch
pedal to the metal,
a custom big bore engine
with a big ass
four barrel carburetor
fully open,
roaring down
dirt roads of the
backcountry,
police didn't have a chance
of stopping him

when booze became
legal again
he opened a distillery
in his garage-
making it
for friends,
cousins,
old customers;
regardless
of where or who
ATF ruled
he can give it
or sell it…
for cash

this is a free country

a hundred years of
Tennessee mountains
ain't changing nothin'
that don't need changin'

you can ask
anybody down
these parts 'bout that

if you ask nicely,
you might even
buy it at The Joint
(it's his cousin's place)

the railroad station

use to be
the train
was the main route
out of the area
if you want to visit
family or friends faraway

the curves of the iron track
glitter in the noon sun
by the long bends
at the end of the platform,
where you can see
the locomotive
pulling into the station
on a sunny day

the conductor hops off,
wearing a jacket and tie
regardless of the heat;
he opens the doors
to pull down steps
so waiting passengers
can climb on board

the wood planked
platform is almost
at ground level,
with a sloping green canopy
offering shade
from the southern sun

if you are sitting
on a bench waiting,
you can see under

the rail cars
right across
to the other side
of the tracks
where feral dogs
congregate;
waiting for the train
to pull out
so they explore for
tossed food scraps
on the station floor,
or near wastebaskets

home

her husband walked out on her-
too many bills,
too many drinks,
too many arguments,
too many demands
to sober up

he left her
with a daughter,
the double wide,
a lot of debt-
she paid the bills
as usual by
working double shifts
while her girlfriend
babysat the little girl
at night and after school

the trailer park is kept neat,
many homes
on their fourth
or fifth owners-
for many, this is the best
they can do at this time

when her cold water pipe
sprung a leak
the park manager was away-
the floor was flooded inches deep;
to remove the water she took
a drill,
made a hole in the floor
for it to drain out,
then threw a small rug on top

in the beginning

growing up on a small farm
singing while feeding chickens
early before school,
then helping
dress and feed her siblings;
she was the oldest
of five in the family

in high school
she was lanky and thin,
some might say skinny,
with long straight hair
flowing down her back
almost to her waist;
always a hello
with a smile on her face

none of the boys
in school interested her;
too close,
too informed of their habits,
old blood to her,
not a fresh face.
then the interschool dance happened

two high schools,
each one from a valley over the ridge
on either side of town
sent kids to the dance

most boys
had flat top haircuts,
cropped close to the ears,
others wore crew cuts,

tight jeans,
white shirts,
except one

he stood
in the entrance
for a moment
wearing blue jeans,
a western shirt
with mother of pearl buttons,
cowboy boots
and long hair
combed back in a ducktail

standing by the wall
with her girlfriends
he approached her,
asked for a dance;
she took his hand,
walked onto the middle
of the basketball court,
then placed her arms
around his neck

when the dance band
stopped for a break
a few boys asked
if they could play instead;
the answer was yes

he walked to the microphone
and started to sing;
then she walked up
and joined in -
the place went crazy

after, she asked where he learned
to sing like that...

The Joint he said

aren't you too young to be in there?

yes,
but the owner lets me sing,
he's an old buddy of my dad;
they grew up together,
they've been in the Klan
for many years - best friends

this is how she started singing
at the joint

ten years later
an agent from Memphis
discovered her one night;
now she tours far and wide
as a major country singer

as usual - Summer

waking before dawn every day
before the alarm clock goes off
she drags herself out of bed,
puts on her boots and clothes then
walks outside to tend the animals

it is a small, hardscrabble farm
located in the shadow of an
overbearing mountain, throwing
shade over the house instead of sun

the widow hears the rooster's welcome-
corn is scattered across the dirt yard
for hens to peck at, field mice
to eat the uneaten kernels, and crows
sitting on the roof of the barn
watching and waiting for their opportunity

the henhouse surrenders fresh eggs to be
sorted, marked, then brought to the local
supermarket to keep the farm going,
sustaining it for now

after decades, nothing has changed-
the barn still holds her husband's
1955 red Chevrolet, drop-cloth covered,
cinderblocks supporting it, forever
waiting for him to unwrap, and
drive away with her into the sunset

sometimes, dreams never happen

fatback

the local Walmart in town
doesn't sell it, but folks here
drive to the locally owned
Piggly Wiggly supermarket
close to town to buy it

a salty southern delight

breakfast, lunch or dinner
it makes the perfect side dish;
or just hang out chewing
fatback on the front porch
while talking with friends

from generation to generation

the school bus stops
to pick up students
in the morning, then
brings them back later

the more rural homes
are scattered away from each other,
so when kids play together
they tend to frolic a long time

the thirteen-year-old girl
frolicked too much in the woods,
like her mother did
thirteen years before

now she watches the bus
drive past her house,
carrying friends to school
each day without her

her future in tatters

that area of town

in whispers…
most folks will talk about it,
the impolite speak in almost hushed tones,
while the more brazen don't hold back

driving through that section of town
you see old men sitting, rocking on
chairs under a slanted porch;
support bricks missing underneath

half naked children playing in the front yard;
torn yellowed shades hanging down
in windows with fans whirring away, trying
to cool off the unbearable heat inside

no reason to visit unless you live there,
or are looking for something illicit-
good folks stay away, just because…
yes, just because of the unspoken reason

it's not a good reason or a valid reason-
it's just reality, human behavior
taught in childhood or learned later on;
hard to change attitudes and ignorance

the big day

she drove to Chattanooga on the interstate
to select a dress for her wedding; to be held
in a church located beside the bubbling creek,
on a rolling hill, just outside of town

her mother, best friend, and sister came along
to help decide on the dress; white of course, not ivory-
the dress shops are too costly, so they check out the
thrift stores associated with local city churches,
until they found the perfect dress

as the piano starts to play the bride enters, escorted by
her father and mother, then the groom follows behind;
wearing a blue suit he bought from Wal-Mart last week,
instead of his usual blue jeans and green John Deere hat

high school sweethearts,
teenagers,
they decided to marry
before the baby came along;
although her friends didn't marry
and remain single parents

after the wedding
they're moving in with her parents
in a small trailer near the barn;
usually used for migrant
field workers in season

both dropping out of school
to start their family

honeymoon fever

Dollywood is not too far away,
locally known as a honeymoon destination
for the five states surrounding it;
next to the Smoky Mountains National Park

coming off the interstate highway
you are on a two lane back country road;
trees and open fields slow down the pace of time,
lulling the driver into a casual country calm

going over a small bridge only feet
above a gently flowing stream,
the road twists and turns, leading the
driver right into the heart of Pigeon Ford

the last right turn on the one lane road
opens into a multi lane main street;
bumper to bumper cars barely moving, with
packed motels on either side of the road,

young adults drinking on balconies,
girls sitting on rooftops of parked pickups,
music blasting from open car windows,
a sign should read welcome to Hillbilly Las Vegas

firehouse barbeque

the first Friday night of each month in summer
the volunteer fire department holds a barbeque,
asking for donations to keep the equipment
up to date and in working order

Fat Momma Alice cooks for everyone
her specialty, Southern Fried Chicken,
with her secret seasoning (finely ground
bacon bits) in the thick, rich batter

plus she only fries in a months' worth
of saved bacon grease. after decades of
this weekend feast, nobody ever thought
why everyone in town has high cholesterol

but they die with a smile
on their face, and a full tummy's worth
of Fat Momma Alice's
bacon fried chicken

Sunday services come weekly

the pews are almost full with just enough space
between worshippers to move their arms a little

fire and brimstone rained down from the altar, covering
each congregant with feelings of repentance… maybe

the wife sitting in the rear with her family is eyeing
her close personal friend sitting with his wife two rows
over

the fifty-year-old gay bachelor in the front is ignoring
the women sitting on his sides who waste their thoughts
on him, not knowing

the wine on the altar is mixed with ten-year-old
bourbon to grease his tongue so the preacher can
be eloquent

finishing the sermon, the words "he who is without
sin…" causes a few folks to mentally squirm in their
seats

leaving religion at the door, they walk to their car
already forgetting what was said only minutes before

small town standout

moaning, starting the sixth hour of labor,
the baby was slow to come out-
finally, the head crowned, gently
a midwife guided the body
until it was firmly in her hands

placing the baby boy on his mother's chest
he would become her only son,
although there were other pregnancies
in the next few years, but they were all girls

in a farming accident, his father died,
raised by his mother, grandmother,
and taking care of his younger sisters
he lived in an all-female home

adored, he loved to dance and sing-
growing up learning to play guitar

in fourth grade, as the year started,
he pirouetted through the door
to the classroom; then they knew-
no one said anything, but they all knew

in high school, he was in all the plays,
choruses, and was a cheerleader too-
until they found his body one morning
in the next town stuffed in a dumpster
behind a rundown ramshackle bar

the law

lonely roads, backcountry woods,
homes scattered far and wide,
the county sheriff's deputies
patrol the area, protecting all

a domestic disturbance dominates
the calls one night; two
deputies from different directions
arrive finding a blood drenched body

a mix of short tempers and alcohol
results in actions which cannot be
withdrawn; too many times
they see this happen over and over

either a gun or knife is the weapon of choice,
usually fists are used; they only result in
disfigured faces, women mainly,
with broken noses and marriages
they leave the home
filling the only safe house
 in the county

so many reasons,
so many lives lost
so many questions
so many unanswered

school

reading, writing, and arithmetic
are taught in heated classrooms
in May and June, no air conditioning,
so sweat-stained papers are handed in

the wooden desks are decades old,
initials carved in the top makes
writing difficult. the dried ink wells
sunk in them make great pencil holders

the teacher's words blend together
as boys daydream about summer,
and tie knots in the long hair
of the girls sitting in front of them

the Scopes Monkey Trial is still being
fought today; evolution is taught
alongside creationism as fact;
as dictated by many school boards

science is a question to be discussed, not a fact.
it need not be backwoods
becoming backwards-
politicians who long for the past
are ignoring the future;
hurting the people who elected them

a red mailbox

the state road runs through
a typical intersection
outside of town,
which has a dead-end street attached

fifty feet down, the thick forest begins
with a solitary red mailbox
pointing to an unpaved road,
which starts winding through
dense stands of tall trees
blocking sightlines
from the highway…only yards away

a short drive ends
in front of a small house
buried beneath
a ceiling of high branches,
blocking the sun outside;
inside, a warm welcoming
to those who know the meaning
of the bright red mail box

nobody ever mentions this house,
or what goes on inside;
just plain folk
going to look at the trees
by the red mailbox-
where boys become men
at the appropriate time in their life-
a legend passed down
from father to son
for generations

cold water

as teenage boys
they knew where the small lake,
hidden in the woods, is located
so they could go swimming
after school let out in June

the hot, humid days of summer
brought them there
after working on a farm
to cool off,
languishing in
the cool shaded water
beneath the tall summer trees;
their clothes piled high on
low hanging branches-
disturbed only by the frogs
and slithering snakes sitting
on sun-drenched rocks on
the other side of the pond

this is a boy only spot,
girls are not allowed-
except late at night,
with a full moon
and on a date;
then they too
can go swimming

all spiffed up

deep undersea
a mollusk hoards
it's bounty,
until divers
swim up with it
throwing oysters
onto a boat

South Sea pearls are
considered so
beautiful,
so expensive,
only the rich like
Rockefellers
can afford them

in Appalachia,
hundreds of miles
from the ocean,
thousands of miles
from the South Seas-
in the middle
of the South,
some ladies wear
pearls when dressing
in their Sunday
best to impress

not natural pearls,
but they look good,
cost a lot less,
look realistic-
and bought at Walmart
for ten dollars

Jesus

a lot of people in these parts believe…
there is a church for every denomination,
they abound just about everywhere
around here; one doesn't have to look too hard

nice to know there are some faith-based
folk who open their hearts to the poor,
the hungry, the people in need of help;
just as its preached Sunday in church

except if you speak Spanish, are fleeing
murderous drug gangs, have dark skin,
are willing to do jobs white people don't
want, and wear everything you own on your back

makes you stop and wonder…
what did Jesus teach?

American whiskey

oak, smoke, smooth,
aged twelve years,
single malt,
triple distilled
black barrel
charcoal taste
Bourbon

other than beer
by the can
or bottle,
the drink of choice
as American
as apple pie
is Bourbon

served in bars,
fine restaurants,
or drinking at home
with others or alone;
is Bourbon

just enough is fine,
not to be drunk
like a fine wine,
too much can cause
a problem for everyone;
jail, divorce, or death

racing

big time events bring big-time crowds-
NASCAR stock cars are anything
but stock cars; souped up with a custom
engineered engine racing at a sanctioned track

heroes are created by the media-
looked up to by small-town teens
who try to emulate the speed
on desolate, narrow, back country roads

some succeed, some don't-
there are trees with missing bark
testifying to the force of cars
crashing into an immoveable obstacle

heroes win trophies,
teens win wheelchairs,
some win dirt
six feet down;
trying to be a hero too

yummy in your tummy

collard greens, cornbread, fried chicken,
okra, fried green tomatoes, grits with shrimp,
cobbler, pecan pie, gumbo, sweet tea, BBQ,
banana pudding, mashed potatoes, ribs,
chicken fried steak, sweet potato pie,
hush puppies, red beans and rice, brisket,
biscuits and gravy, and pralines

where to start?
when to stop?
hand or fork?
it's all good

lunch

Valley Bar and Grill is down the block
from the courthouse, sitting next to
the large County parking lot

Sis has been employed at the court
as a clerical since high school;
waking up with the roosters
to shower and put on her makeup
before leaving for work

at lunch, she sits at the end
of the bar draped in shadows
from poor lighting
covering her facial lines
of past experiences,
drooping jowls, and a past
not many know about-
eating and relaxing,
while watching the lawyers
enter with their clients;
the only quiet place
to eat in town

one dead husband, another who
abandoned her, two ex-boyfriends,
and now a quiet social life
except for two nights a week;
when a presiding judge
drives her to Chattanooga
for dinner at the expensive
Summerhill Hotel, then back
in time for court the next morning

visiting New Jersey

her girlfriend's husband
is traveling up north
on business;
she was asked
to tag along for the ride
to keep her company

mid-twenties,
petite,
blond with a long ponytail,
wearing tight pants
and a print blouse-
she is cute,
a single mother

at lunch with everyone
she asks the cient,
with a smile
and a twinkle in her eye,
if he would like to take
her shopping?

he declines,
but his single son
asks to take her out
for dinner

they hit it off

a week later
she's back home-
they talk on the phone
and the conversation flows

she asks
what church do you go to

*i don't,
i'm Jewish*

*oh…i don't think my daddy
would like that;
he's in the klan!*

she is still single

farm life

as the sun comes up
over the mountain's crest
life begins to stir
on the farm,
roosters crowing,
pigs trampling around
in the muck,
chickens
coming out of the coop
looking for scattered corn,
while the tractor is started
coughing out
diesel exhaust
while rumbling to the field
to begin
the day's work
plowing and
turning the field

the kids gather
the eggs
then throw feed
into the pig trough
while their mother
gets ready to drive to town for work

the farm turns a profit
after paying the mortgage
and business loans;
but to get the extras in life
his wife works in a church in town

Sunday is church,
dress up day,

sitting in the pews
while the preacher rattles on
everyone listens,
then forgets what he said
once they go back home

when the service is finished,
congregants gone,
the music director leaves her
baton in the preacher's office-
as they hug and embrace
with a passionate kiss,
while the farmer waits
for her in the car outside

Effie's House of Beauty - a true story

located on a side street
off the square
she rents space
from the funeral parlor
with her own entrance
in the parking lot;
after many years
a following developed

a new customer
is sitting in the chair,
asks Effie
*if it bothered her to work
in the same building
as a funeral home;
what with all
the dead bodies coming in*

*not at all.
there's even an unclaimed
body in the basement;
want to see it?*
with an affirmative
nod of the head,
the two women
leave to explore

once downstairs Effie brings her
to an upright body
leaning against the wall-
that's LeRoy! she shouted
*my long lost brother-in-law!
he disappeared twenty years ago!*

uniting families

although both families
lived in the same county
for more generations
then anyone can remember,
no one is sure
how the never-ending
feud began;
nor how it is ever going
to be resolved

only two valley's
from each other;
numerous times
law enforcement
became involved
to quiet things down
when they met
at a county fair or
sporting event

finally one morning
the state police
are called

two teenagers
are reported missing,
a boy and a girl-
one from each family,
the boy's car
is gone too

no one
had any idea
they were dating

until a call came in
to the girl's mother,
they eloped-
driving to South Carolina
to marry; she was pregnant

it took time,
but a baby
healed the rift
that could not
be healed
for generations

small town sports

big time professional sports
are not too popular
in the backwater
towns of the South

high school football
drives the conversation
in the fall and winter
when locals meet

a state championship banner
hanging
in the school gymnasium,
with the trophy
all lite up
in the glass showcase
in the main entrance lobby
is a significant point of pride

the field at night comes alive
with parents and graduates
in the bleachers
cheering on
the clash of young bodies-
smashing into one another,
gritting their teeth,
plowing ahead
for another inch of ground
to win…
and play another day,
another round,
in the tournament
for the state banner
to hang high

broken bones
torn ligaments
fractures too numerous-
injuries they will carry
till the day they die…
for a flag to hang high
for fifty plus years

the player's names,
and faces forgotten
in the fog of history

the end